My Sp Words

Consultants

Ashley Bishop, Ed.D.

Sue Bishop, M.E.D.

Publishing Credits

Dona Herweck Rice, *Editor-in-Chief*

Robin Erickson, *Production Director*

Lee Aucoin, *Creative Director*

Sharon Coan, *Project Manager*

Jamey Acosta, *Editor*

Rachelle Cracchiolo, M.A.Ed., *Publisher*

Image Credits

cover and Eric Isselée/Shutterstock; p.3 orionmystery@flickr/Shutterstock; p.4 eddtoro/Shutterstock; p.5 Noel Powell, Schaumburg/Shutterstock; p.6 pigscanfly/Bigstock; p.7 lostbear/Bigstock; p.8 Danny Smythe/Bigstock; p.9 Chepe Nicoli/Dreamstime; p.10 JamesWooten/Bigstock; back cover pigscanfly/Bigstock

Teacher Created Materials

5301 Oceanus Drive
Huntington Beach, CA 92649-1030
http://www.tcmpub.com

ISBN 978-1-4333-3984-4

© 2012 Teacher Created Materials, Inc.
Printed in China

Look at the spider.

Where is the spider?

Look at the **spacesuit**

Where is the **sp**acesuit?

Look at the sponge.

Where is the **sp**onge?

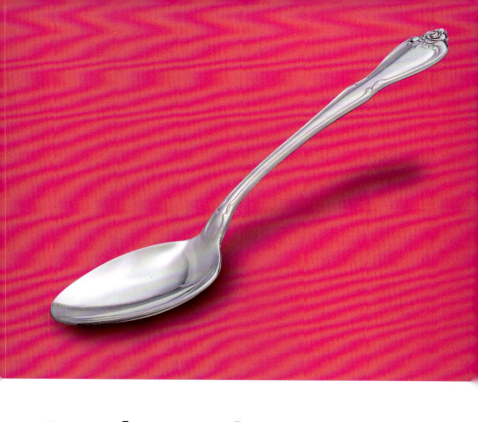

Look at the sp‌oon.

Where is the spoon?

Look at the spaghetti

Glossary

spacesuit **sp**aghetti **sp**ider

sponge **sp**oon

Sight Words

Look   at   the   Where   is

Activities

- Read the book aloud to your child, pointing to the *sp* words. Help your child describe where the *sp* objects are found.

- Discuss the differences between a spoon and other eating utensils (fork, knife, chop sticks). Ask your child to name foods he or she eats with a spoon.

- Teach your child "The Itsy Bitsy Spider." Hold your thumbs in and pretend your fingers are spider legs. Ask your child to count the number of legs.

- Cut shapes out of sponges and allow your child to make a sponge painting, using water-based paints.

- Help your child think of a personally valuable word to represent the letters *sp*, such as *sport*.